CROCHET
Granny Square
TOPS, BAGS, AND MORE

SALENA BACA

STACKPOLE BOOKS

Essex, Connecticut
Blue Ridge Summit,
Pennsylvania

STACKPOLE BOOKS

An imprint of The Globe Pequot Publishing Group, Inc.
64 South Main Street
Essex, CT 06426
www.globepequot.com

Distributed by NATIONAL BOOK NETWORK
800-462-6420

Photography by Jason Kennedy, jkennedyphotography.com

We have made every effort to ensure the accuracy and completeness of these instructions. We cannot, however, be responsible for human error, typographical mistakes, or variations in individual work.

British Library Cataloguing in Publication Information available

Library of Congress Cataloging-in-Publication Data available

ISBN 978-0-8117-7532-8 (paper : alk. paper)
ISBN 978-0-8117-7533-5 (electronic)

♾™ The paper used in this publication meets the minimum requirements of American National Standard for Information Sciences—Permanence of Paper for Printed Library Materials, ANSI/NISO Z39.48-1992.

First Edition

Contents

Newsboy Hat
11

Cowl
13

Hooded Scarf
15

Scrap Bag
18

Tote
19

Market Tote
21

Shrug
23

Button Front Top
25

Basic Stitch Poncho
27

Side-Split Top
29

Introduction

Ever heard of a granny square? Probably the most iconic crochet motif, it is the perfect starting point for making anything from a cozy afghan to modern accessories.

A granny square starts from the center and builds outward, creating a pattern of double crochet stitches and chain spaces that form a uniquely distinct square. While there are quite a few ways to crochet a granny square, I've got a set of instructions to share that are my absolute favorite. And with these, you can follow every pattern in this collection like a crochet champ!

This collection is here to show the world that granny squares aren't just for grandmas anymore—they're a blank canvas for your crochet dreams. You can personalize them in so many different ways and turn them into bags, accessories, and even fashionable clothing.

In this book, I'll walk you through every round to crochet these squares separately (or join them together) to create a fantastic array of granny square projects that I know you'll love.

Long live the crochet granny square!

Peace + Love + Crochet,
Salena Baca

Abbreviations

BLO = back loop only

ch(s) = chain(s)

dc = double crochet

FPdc = front post double crochet

FPhdc = front post half double crochet

JAYGO = join as you go

sc = single crochet

Sl st = slip stitch

st(s) = stitch(es)

Crochet a Granny Square

GRANNY SQUARE TIPS

As popular as they are, these iconic square motifs are really not a beginner-friendly pattern to crochet because of their complex repeat symbols and stitch arrangements. But they are far from impossible! I'll walk you through the first few rounds to success; just follow my simple instructions, pattern chart, and photo tutorials to help you with every step.

If this is your first time crocheting a granny square, be sure to use the following tips.

TIP 1: Practice First

Before you jump hook-first into a granny square project in this collection, pick up some scrap yarn and follow the instructions for just one motif, working up at least four rounds. This will give you the confidence and practice you need to follow any other pattern here.

TIP 2: Follow the Instructions in Small Steps

Because granny squares are worked in joined rounds to create a square shape, we must get a little fancy with the repeat symbols. To get the hang of them, follow the instructions like this: read each line, follow the instruction to the comma, and then check that your stitches match each line and the final stitch count. With those tips in mind, this may be an easier way to consider the instructions.

TIP 3: Use the Pattern Chart

As we just saw, granny square instructions can be a bit complex to read and follow. Sometimes just reading instructions can be tricky to follow and understand, so be sure to use the pattern chart on page 7 for this motif for guidance.

Start in the center, then find the starting chain. Moving one stitch at a time, identify the stitches in the order they are worked for round 1, ending with the slip stitch. Match the stitch arrangement with the written instructions. Match the final stitch count with the written instructions. Repeat for rounds 2 through 4.

TIP 4: Good Practice Makes Great Progress

What I love most about granny squares is their versatility; they can turn into bags, hats, scarves, tops . . . they really can do a lot!

Granny squares also do a great job of hiding some beginner flaws like uneven tension and color changes, so you can relax knowing that every motif you make will create a great project that you'll love.

Remember, practice makes progress, and these projects are a fantastic way to build up your crochet knowledge, skills, and confidence.

Round 1 (Right Side):
Ch 4 (first dc + base ch),
skip 3 ch,
Note: Work the remaining instructions into the base ch (4th ch from hook).
2 dc,
[ch 3, 3 dc] 3 times,
ch 3,
Sl st into top of beginning ch-3 to join.
—24 sts; 12 dc + 4 ch-3 spaces.

Round 2:
Sl st into each of next 2 dc,
Sl st into ch-3 space,
ch 3 (first dc),
(2 dc, ch 3, 3 dc) into same ch-3 space,
ch 1,
[(3 dc, ch 3, 3 dc) into next ch-3 space,
ch 1] 3 times,
Sl st into top of beginning ch-3 to join.
—40 sts; 24 dc + 4 ch-3 spaces + 4 ch-1 spaces.

TIP 5: Measure Granny Squares

Not every granny square you crochet has to exactly match the stitch and row gauge listed (like the tote bags in this book). But projects that will be worn should be a close match, so getting the gauge of your fabric to match the pattern will be important.

Granny squares are worked in joined rounds from the center out, so you can measure them a few different ways depending on the type of project you're creating.

Here are how different parts of a granny square can be measured:

Measure Rows

To measure the height of rows, start in the center of the granny square at the base of the first row, then measure to the last row worked. You can also measure the height of rows by measuring from side to side.

Measure the height of rows by starting at the base of the first row and measuring to the last row worked.

Measure the height of rows by measuring from side to side.

Measure Stitches

To measure the width of stitches, start in the center of a chain 3 corner and then measure to any adjacent chain 3 corner. Just like measuring rows, you can also measure the width of stitches by measuring from side to side.

And when the pattern gauge notes the square measurement (example: 5 rows = 4 in./10 cm square), you'll measure across any one side after the indicated number of rows are complete.

To measure the width of stitches, start in the center of a chain 3 corner and then measure to any adjacent chain 3 corner.

Measure Diagonally

Unless a pattern says to measure diagonally, this is not typically how to gauge the size of a granny square. Just as a reference however, you can measure the Market Tote (page 21) this way because two of the three motifs will be folded diagonally, which will create the height.

Diagonal measurements may be used for the Market Tote (page 21).

Now, let's go make some granny squares!

GRANNY SQUARE PATTERN

Round 1 (right side): Ch 4 (first dc + base ch), skip 3 ch, 2 dc, [ch 3, 3 dc] 3 times, ch 3, Sl st into top of beginning ch-3 (first dc) to join—24 sts; 12 dc + 4 ch-3 spaces.

Round 1

Round 2: Sl st into each of next 2 dc, Sl st into ch-3 space, ch 3, (2 dc, ch 3, 3 dc) into same ch-3 space, ch 1, [(3 dc, ch 3, 3 dc) into next ch-3 space, ch 1] 3 times, Sl st into top of beginning ch-3 to join—40 sts; 24 dc + 4 ch-3 spaces + 4 ch-1 spaces.

Beginning Round 2   *Round 2*

Round 3: Sl st into each of next 2 dc, Sl st into ch-3 space, ch 3, (2 dc, ch 3, 3 dc) into same ch-3 space, ch 1, (3 dc, ch 1) into ch-1 space, [(3 dc, ch 3, 3 dc) into next ch-3 space, ch 1, (3 dc, ch 1) into ch-1 space] 3 times, Sl st into top of beginning ch-3 to join—56 sts; 36 dc + 4 ch-3 spaces + 8 ch-1 spaces.

Beginning Round 3   *Round 3*

Round 4: Sl st into each of next 2 dc, Sl st into ch-3 space, ch 3, (2 dc, ch 3, 3 dc) into same ch-3 space, ch 1, (3 dc, ch 1) into each ch-1 space, [(3 dc, ch 3, 3 dc) into next ch-3 space, ch 1, (3 dc, ch 1) into each ch-1 space] 3 times, Sl st into top of beginning ch-3 to join—72 sts; 48 dc + 4 ch-3 spaces + 12 ch-1 spaces.

Round 4 can be repeated as many times as needed per pattern instructions, which will add 16 sts (12 dc + 4 ch) to each new round of work.

Beginning Round 4   *Round 4*

Stitch Key

 Chain   **1, 2, etc.** Row Number

• Slip Stitch   Double Crochet

Granny Square Motif Chart

GRANNY SQUARE JOINS

When a project calls for more than one granny square joined together, there are quite a few options for you to try. While a crochet pattern will outline how a project should be joined together, here are some of my favorite joining techniques, which are also referenced in this collection of patterns.

JAYGO Join

JAYGO (join as you go) is a technique that seamlessly joins the current granny square with a previously formed granny square (the joining motif). While JAYGO can be worked in a few ways, these instructions **replace a chain in the current granny square with a slip stitch into the joining motif.**

To incorporate JAYGO into the pattern instructions, follow these steps:

1. First, work the current granny square (right) a full round smaller than the joining motif (left), and ensure all fabric is facing the same direction.

Left to right: Joining motif, current granny square

2. Next, continue the pattern instructions on the final round for the current granny square (right), except JAYGO from ch-3 space to ch-3 space across one or more sides of the joining motif (left). Note that the ch-3 corner instructions say to [ch 1, JAYGO, ch 1], to make the join and ch-3 space even.

JAYGO in ch-3 corner.

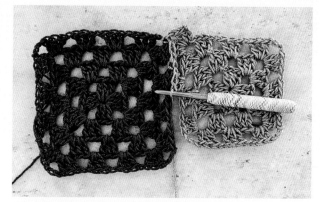

JAYGO in ch-3 corner, next ch-1 space.

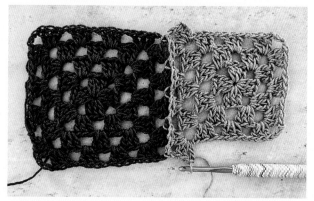

JAYGO in ch-3 corner, next 3 ch-1 spaces, ch-3 corner.

JAYGO across 1 side, final round of current granny square complete per pattern instructions.

Don't overthink this! This method might seem tricky, but it is a really simple way to join granny squares together seamlessly.

Slip Stitch Join

Slip stitches create a thick, sturdy seam by working through two granny squares at a time along their outer edges.

To use a slip stitch seam, just follow these steps:

1. First, all granny squares that should be joined must have the same number of rounds. Note that your yarn should typically match the fabric to hide the seam, but this example shows a contrast for reference.

Granny squares ready to be joined

2. Next, making sure each square is facing the same direction, from chain-3 corner to chain-3 corner, use stitch markers to evenly hold the sides that should be joined together in place.

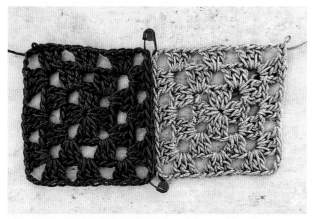

Use stitch markers to hold the sides to be joined together.

3. Then, going through just one loop from each square (the ones touching, in the center) slip stitch the two sides of the squares together from chain-3 corner to chain-3 corner.

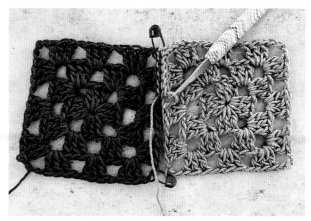

Slip stitch together one loop from each square from corner to corner to join.

This is a great method when you're looking for a thick, sturdy seam. Just be sure to have an even tension that is not too tight as you work this technique.

Completed slip stitch join

Button Front Top

The slip stitch join is also advantageous for joining different types of fabric together, like a granny square edge to a single crochet and chain edge for the Basic Stitch Poncho (page 27), or the granny square edge to the single crochet edge for the Button Front Top (page 25).

Sewn Join

Sewing with a yarn needle will create a flexible seam by working a strand of yarn through two pieces of fabric at a time along their outer edges.

To sew a seam, just follow these steps:

1. First, thread a yarn needle with at least three times the length of yarn as the area to seam. Note that your yarn should typically match the fabric to hide the seam, but this example shows a contrast for reference.

2. Next, making sure all fabric is facing the same direction, use stitch markers to evenly hold the outermost stitches that should be joined together.

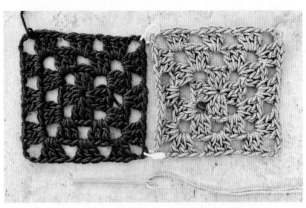

Hold pieces to join together with stitch markers.

3. Then, use a yarn needle to evenly go through both loops for both pieces of fabric that should be joined together. For a uniform seam, always insert the needle from the right side and out through the left side.

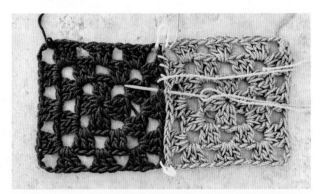

Always insert needle from the right to the left as you join.

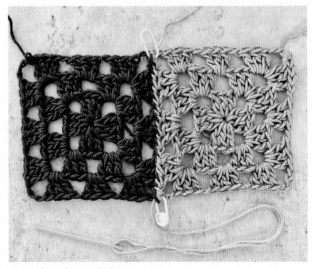

Completed sewn join

Newsboy Hat

FINISHED MEASUREMENTS
23 in./58.5 cm around x 8.5 in./21.5 cm tall with US K-10½ (6.5 mm) hook
25 in./63.5 cm around x 9.5 in./24.25 cm tall with US L-11 (8.0 mm) hook

YARN
Lion Brand Yarn Hue + Me, bulky #5 weight (80% acrylic, 20% wool; 4.4 oz./125 g; 137 yds./125 m): smaller hat in Whisper, 1 skein; larger hat in Saffron, 1 skein

HOOKS AND OTHER MATERIALS
For 23 in./58.5 cm hat: US K-10½ (6.5 mm) crochet hook
For 25 in./63.5 cm hat: US L-11 (8.0 mm) crochet hook
Yarn needle

GAUGE
With US K-10½ (6.5 mm) hook: Round 4 of granny square = 5.5 in./14 cm across
With US L-11 (8.0 mm) hook: Round 4 of granny square = 6.5 in./16.5 cm across

SPECIALTY STITCHES AND TECHNIQUES
BLO = back loop only
FPhdc (front post half double crochet) = Yarn over, insert hook around stitch post (from front to back to front), yarn over, pull back around stitch post, yarn over, pull through 3 loops on hook.

PATTERN NOTE
One set of instructions is given, but two sizes can be worked depending on the crochet hook size used: US K-10½ (6.5 mm) hook for 23 in./58.5 cm hat or US L-11 (8.0 mm) hook for 25 in./63.5 cm hat.

Larger size in Saffron

INSTRUCTIONS (BOTH SIZES)

Use US K-10½ (6.5 mm) crochet hook for 23 in./58.5 cm size, US L-11 (8.0 mm) crochet hook for 25 in./ 63.5 cm size.

Follow Granny Square Instructions (page 7) until 4 rounds are complete.

Rounds 5–9: Sl st into each of next 2 dc, Sl st into ch-1 space, ch 3, (2 dc, ch 1) into same space, (3 dc, ch 1) into each ch-1 space around, Sl st into top of beginning ch-3 to join—64 sts; 48 dc + 16 ch.

Repeat round 5 until 9 rounds are complete, do not fasten off.

Round 10: Ch 1 (not a st, here and throughout), work 1 sc into each st around, Sl st into top of first st to join—64 sc.

Rounds 11–14: Ch 1, FPhdc into each of next 20 sts, Sl st into BLO into each of next 44 sts, Sl st into top of first st to join—64 sts; 20 FPhdc + 44 Sl st.

Repeat round 11 until 14 rounds are complete, fasten off.

Sew in all ends, trim excess.

Smaller size in Whisper

Cowl

FINISHED MEASUREMENTS
25 in./63.5 cm around (center) x 8 in./20.25 cm tall

YARN
Lion Brand Yarn Landscapes Renewed, medium
#4 weight (75% polyester, 25% recycled polyester;
5.3 oz./150 g; 232 yds./212 m): Dreamcatcher, 1 skein

HOOK AND OTHER MATERIALS
US I-9 (5.5 mm) crochet hook
Yarn needle

GAUGE
4 Granny Square rounds = 5 in./12.75 cm square

SPECIALTY STITCHES AND TECHNIQUES
FPdc (front post double crochet) = Yarn over, insert
the hook around the post of the next stitch from front
to back to front, and work a double crochet around the
post.
JAYGO (join as you go) = Replace 1 chain stitch with 1
slip stitch into the joining motif as described on page 8.

PATTERN NOTES
- Pattern is worked in sections: Cowl, Border.
- Refer to first 3 rounds of stitch pattern on motif chart
  on page 7.
- Diagram showing joining order and pattern sections
  is on page 14.
- The border rounds are only worked around double
  crochet stitches from sides of Granny Squares to
  create a tapered style.

▤ INSTRUCTIONS

Cowl

Granny Square 1

Follow Granny Square Instructions on page 7 until 4 rounds are complete, fasten off.

Granny Squares 2–4

Follow same instructions for Granny Square through round 3, then continue to round 4 below to join the first side of the current Granny Square to the third side of the previous Granny Square (leaving 3 sides unjoined).

Round 4: Follow instructions for round 4, except replace second ch along two consecutive ch-3 spaces and each ch-1 space between those spaces with JAYGO, fasten off—72 sts; 48 dc + 4 ch-3 spaces + 12 ch-1 spaces.

Granny Square 5

Follow instructions for Granny Square 1 through round 3, then continue to round 4 below to join the current Granny Square to:

1. third side of the previous Granny Square and
2. first side of the first Granny Square (leaving 2 parallel sides joined and 2 parallel sides unjoined).

Round 4: Follow instructions for Granny Square round 4, except replace second ch along two consecutive ch-3 spaces and each ch-1 space between those spaces with JAYGO, repeat to join into previous Granny Square, then first Granny Square, fasten off—72 sts; 48 dc + 4 ch-3 spaces + 12 ch-1 spaces.

Border

With right sides of Granny Squares facing, attach yarn around any unjoined dc from last round of Cowl.

Round 1 (right side): Ch 1 (not a st, here and throughout), work 1 FPdc around every dc, Sl st into top of first st to join—60 FPdc.

Round 2: Ch 1, work 1 FPdc around each FPdc around, Sl st into top of first st to join.

Repeat round 2 until 3 rounds are complete, fasten off.

With right sides of Granny Squares facing, attach yarn around any unjoined dc from last round of Cowl, opposite Border.

Follow instructions for Border rounds 1 and 2.

Finishing

Sew in all ends, trim excess.

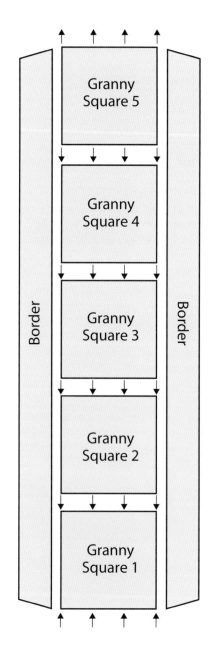

Hooded Scarf

FINISHED MEASUREMENTS
Including Border rounds.
Scarf: 65 in./165 cm long x 9 in./22.75 cm wide
Hood: 11 in./28 cm tall x 22 in./56 cm around

YARN
Lion Brand Yarn Mandala Impressions, bulky #5 weight
(100% acrylic; 5.3 oz./150 g; 164 yds./150 m): Nightfall,
4 cakes

HOOK AND OTHER MATERIALS
US K-10½ (6.5 mm) crochet hook
Stitch markers
Yarn needle

GAUGE
8 Granny Square rounds = 11 in./28 cm square
6 Granny Square rounds = 8 in./20.25 cm square

SPECIALTY STITCHES AND TECHNIQUES
JAYGO (join as you go) = Replace 1 chain stitch with 1
slip stitch into the joining motif as described on page 8.
Sew = Use yarn needle to join (sew) pieces of fabric
together as described on page 10.

PATTERN NOTE
Pattern is worked in sections: Scarf, Hood, Border.

INSTRUCTIONS

Scarf

Granny Square 1
Follow Granny Square Instructions on page 7 until 6
    rounds are complete, adding 16 sts to each new
    round of work, ending with 104 sts, fasten off—4
    ch-3 spaces + 72 dc + 20 ch-1 spaces.

Granny Squares 2–8
Follow Granny Square instructions through round 5,
    then continue to round 6 (next page) to join the
    first side of the current Granny Square to the third
    side of the previous Granny Square (leaving 3 sides
    unjoined).

Round 6: Follow instructions for round 4, except replace second ch along two consecutive ch-3 spaces and each ch-1 space between those spaces with JAYGO, fasten off—104 sts; 4 ch-3 spaces + 72 dc + 20 ch-1 spaces.

Hood

Granny Square 1
Follow Granny Square instructions until 8 rounds are complete, adding 16 sts to each new round of work, ending with 136 sts, fasten off—4 ch-3 spaces + 96 dc + 28 ch-1 spaces.

Granny Square 2
Follow instructions for Scarf: Granny Square 1 through 7 rounds, ending with 120 sts—4 ch-3 spaces + 84 dc + 24 ch-1 spaces.

Continue to round 8 below to join sides one and two of current Granny Square to previous Granny Square along sides one and two (leaving 2 consecutive sides joined and 2 unjoined).

Round 8: Follow instructions for round 4, except replace second ch along three consecutive ch-3 spaces and each ch-1 space between those spaces with JAYGO, fasten off—104 sts; 4 ch-3 spaces + 72 dc + 20 ch-1 spaces.

With right sides of Scarf and Hood facing the same direction, evenly align seam of Hood Granny Squares 1 and 2 with seam of Scarf Granny Squares 4 and 5.

Use stitch markers to hold unjoined sides of Hood evenly along sides of Scarf.

With yarn needle, sew two unjoined sides of Hood along center of Scarf. Fasten off.

Border

With right side of Granny Square 1 of Scarf facing, attach yarn into ch-3 space.

Round 1 (right side): Ch 1 (not a st), (sc, ch 3, sc, ch 1) into each ch-3 space, (skip 1 st, sc, ch 1) across sides of Scarf and Hood including Sl st joins between Granny Squares, Sl st into top of first sc to join—488 sts; 240 sc + 248 ch.

Round 2: Ch 1 (not a st), (sc, ch 3, sc, ch 1) into each ch-3 space, (sc, ch 1) into each sc, Sl st into top of first sc to join, fasten off—508 sts; 248 sc + 260 ch.

Tassel (make 5)

Create 1 tassel for each ch-3 space of Border (4 total) and for ch-3 space on back of Hood (1 total).

Cut 1 piece of yarn measuring 12 in./30.5 cm. Fold in half. Loop and knot into ch-3 space.

Cut 10 pieces of yarn measuring 12 in./30.5 cm each (tassel bunch).

Place tassel bunch between knotted strands, then knot strands together again at center of tassel bunch.

Cut 20 in./50.75 strand of yarn; wrap around tassel bunch 1 in./2.5 cm below knot. Knot, tuck ends into tassel.

Trim tassel ends to even, as desired.

Finishing
Sew in all ends, trim excess.

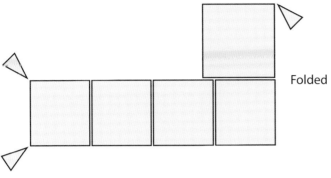

| Granny Square, Hood 1 | Granny Square, Hood 2 |

| Granny Square, Scarf 1 | Granny Square, Scarf 2 | Granny Square, Scarf 3 | Granny Square, Scarf 4 | Granny Square, Scarf 5 | Granny Square, Scarf 6 | Granny Square, Scarf 7 | Granny Square, Scarf 8 |

Folded

Scrap Bag

FINISHED MEASUREMENTS
Tote: 19 in./48.25 cm flat, 38 in./96.5 cm around, 18 in./45.75 cm tall (without handles)
Handles: 16 in./40.75 cm long

YARN
Lion Brand Yarn Lazy Days, medium #4 weight (100% polyester; 3.5 oz./100 g; 179 yds./164 m): Taupe, 2 skeins; Clay, 1 skein

HOOK AND OTHER MATERIALS
US G-6 (4.0 mm) crochet hook
Scissors

GAUGE
7 Granny Square rounds = 4 in./10.25 cm square

PATTERN NOTES
- Pattern is worked in one piece from the bottom up, working in joined rounds.
- Change color as desired, or follow change sequence shown in this example:
    Rounds 1–4, 6–9, 11–14, 16–19, 21–24, 26–29: Taupe
    Rounds 5, 10, 15, 20, 25, 30–37: Clay

INSTRUCTIONS

Follow Granny Square instructions on page 7 until 10 rounds are complete.

Rounds 11–29: Sl st into each of next 2 dc, Sl st into ch space, ch 3, (2 dc, ch 1) into same ch space, (3 dc, ch 1) into each ch space around, Sl st into top of beginning ch-3 to join—160 sts; 120 dc + 40 ch-1 spaces.

Repeat round 11 until 29 rounds are complete.

Round 30: Sl st into each of next 2 dc, Sl st into ch space, ch 3, work 2 dc into same ch space, work 3 dc into each ch-1 space around, Sl st into top of beginning ch-3 to join—120 dc.

Rounds 31–32: Ch 1 (not a st), work 1 sc into each st around, Sl st into top of beginning sc to join—120 sc.

Round 33: Ch 1, [work 1 sc into next 30 sts, ch 60, skip 30 sts] 2 times, Sl st into top of beginning sc to join—180 sts; 60 sc + 120 ch.

Rounds 34–36: Ch 1 (not a st), work 1 sc into each st around, Sl st into top of beginning sc to join—180 sc.

Round 37: Sl st into each st around, fasten off—180 Sl sts.

Sew in all ends, trim excess.

Tote

FINISHED MEASUREMENTS
Tote: 13 in./33 cm flat, 26 in./66 cm around, 14.5 in./36.75 cm tall (without handles)
Handles: 20 in./50.75 cm long

YARN
Lion Brand Yarn 24/7 Cotton, medium #4 weight (100% cotton; 3.5 oz./100 g; 186 yds./170 m): Tangerine, Camel, Navy, Ecru, Hay Bale, and Goldenrod; 1 bag = 372 total yds./340.2 m
See Pattern Notes for exact sequence used in the example pictured.

HOOK AND OTHER MATERIALS
US G-6 (4.0 mm) crochet hook
Scissors

GAUGE
4 Granny Square rounds = 4.5 in./11.5 cm square

SPECIALTY TECHNIQUE
JAYGO (join as you go) = Replace 1 chain stitch with 1 slip stitch into the joining motif as described on page 8.

PATTERN NOTES
- Pattern is worked in sections: Square 1, Square 2, Handles.
- Change color as desired or follow change sequence show in the example, as below:

  Square 1
  Rounds 1–2: Tangerine
  Rounds 3–4: Camel
  Rounds 5–6: Navy
  Rounds 7–8, 13: Ecru
  Rounds 9–10: Hay Bale
  Rounds 11–12: Goldenrod

  Square 2
  Rounds 1–2, 5–6, 9–10, 13: Ecru
  Rounds 3–4, 11–12: Camel
  Rounds 7–8: Hay Bale

  Handles
  Rounds 1–6: Ecru

Square 1

With first JAYGO, ensure wrong sides of Square 1 and Square 2 are held together on the inside of the bag (right sides each facing on the outside of the bag).

Round 13: Sl st into each of next 2 dc, Sl st into ch-3 space, ch 3, (2 dc, ch 1, JAYGO into any ch-3 space of Square 1, ch 1, 3 dc) into same ch-3 space, *JAYGO into next ch-1 space of Square 1, [work 3 dc into next ch-1 space of Square 2, JAYGO into next ch-1 space of Square 1] 11 times, (3 dc, ch 1, JAYGO into next ch-3 space of Square 1, ch 1, 3 dc) into ch-3 space,* work from * to * 3 times total, [ch 1, (3 dc, ch 1)] into next 11 ch-1 spaces, Sl st into top of beginning ch-3 to join—216 sts; 156 dc + 20 ch + 40 Sl st.

Do not fasten off; continue to Handles.

Handles

Round 1 (right side): Sl st into each of next 2 dc, Sl st into ch, Sl st into JAYGO, ch 1 (not a st, here and throughout), work 1 sc into each of next 14 sts,* ch 70, skip 27 sts, sc into each of next 13 sts*, sc into JAYGO, sc into each of next 13 sts, work from * to * 1 more time, Sl st into top of first sc to join—194 sts; 54 sc + 140 ch.

Round 2: Ch 1, work 1 sc into each st around, Sl st into top of first sc to join—194 sc.

Repeat round 2 until 5 rounds are complete. Fasten off.

Finishing

Sew in all ends, trim excess.

Square 2

INSTRUCTIONS

Granny Square 1

Follow Granny Square instructions on page 7 until 13 rounds are complete, adding 16 sts to each new round of work, ending with 216 sts, fasten off—4 ch-3 spaces + 156 dc + 48 ch-1 spaces.

Granny Square 2

Follow Granny Square instructions until 12 rounds are complete, do not fasten off. Round 13 of Square 2 will evenly join into Square 1 across 3 sides using JAYGO method (see Specialty Technique).

Market Tote

FINISHED MEASUREMENTS
Tote: 20 in./50.75 cm across x 20 in./50.75 cm tall

YARN
Lion Brand Yarn 24/7 Cotton, medium #4 weight (100% mercerized cotton; 3.5 oz./100 g; 186 yds./170 m per): Ecru, 3 skeins; also shown in Beets and Hay Bale

HOOK AND OTHER MATERIALS
US G-6 (4.0 mm) crochet hook
Scissors

GAUGE
1 Square = 14 in./35.5 cm square

SPECIALTY TECHNIQUE
JAYGO (join as you go) = Replace 1 chain stitch with 1 slip stitch into the joining motif as described on page 8.

PATTERN NOTES
- Tote is created in sections: Squares (3), Handle, Border.
- Use Granny Square diagram on page 7 as a guide when following Round 13 for Granny Square 3.

INSTRUCTIONS

Squares 1 and 2
Follow Granny Square instructions on page 7 until 13 rounds are complete. Fasten off.

Square 3
Follow Granny Square instructions until 12 rounds are complete. Round 13 will be worked with JAYGO, joining Square 1 into two sides of Square 1 and two sides of Square 2. Ensure right sides of all three squares are facing the same direction as they are joined together.

Worked in Beets and Hay Bale

Round 13: Follow instructions for round 4, except:

Replace second ch from ch-3 between sides 4 and 1 with JAYGO into Granny Square 2, then Granny Square 1.

Replace each ch-1 space on sides 1 and 2 with JAYGO into ch-1 spaces of Granny Square 1.

Replace second ch from ch-3 between sides 2 and 3 with JAYGO into Granny Square 1, then Granny Square 2.

Replace each ch-1 space on sides 3 and 4 with JAYGO into ch-1 spaces of Granny Square 2—216 sts; 156 dc + 4 ch-3 spaces + 48 ch-1 spaces.

Handle

With right side facing, attach yarn into first ch in open ch-3 corner for Granny Square 1.

Row 1: Ch 1 (not a st, here and throughout), work 1 sc into each ch across—3 sc.

Row 2: Ch 1, turn, work 1 sc into each st across—3 sc.

Repeat row 2 until 25 rows are complete.

Row 26: Ch 1, turn, [Sl st through both loops of last row and ch in open ch-3 corner for Granny Square 2] across row, fasten off—3 Sl sts.

Border

With right side facing, attach yarn into any ch-1 space on Granny Square 1.

Round 1: Work 1 Sl st into every st around Square 1, sides of sts on Handle, and every st around Square 2, fasten off.

Worked in Ecru

Repeat all Border instructions for opposite side.

Finishing

Sew in all ends, trim excess.

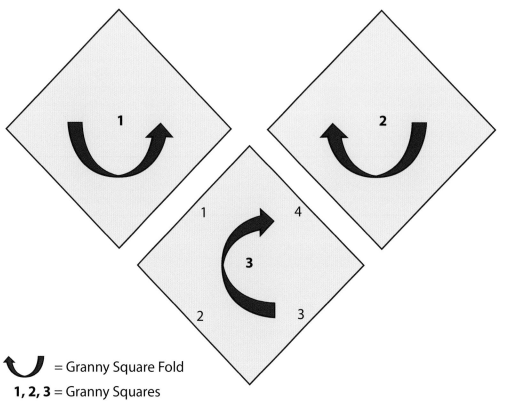

= Granny Square Fold

1, 2, 3 = Granny Squares

1, 2, 3, 4 = Granny Square Sides

Shrug

FINISHED MEASUREMENTS

Back square = Granny Square before sleeves. Wide = total length from sleeve to sleeve.

Small: 28 in./71 cm back square x 54 in./137.25 cm wide

Medium: 33 in./83.75 cm back square x 59 in./149.75 cm wide

Large: 38 in./96.5 cm back square x 64 in./162.5 cm wide

YARN

Lion Brand Yarn Re-Up Bonus Bundle, medium #4 weight (70% recycled cotton, 30% recycled polyester; 14 oz./397 g; 651 yds./595 m): Mineral Springs, 651 (805, 973) yds./595 (736.1, 889.7) m

HOOK AND OTHER MATERIALS

US M-13 (9.0 mm) crochet hook

Stitch markers

Yarn needle

GAUGE

3 Granny Square rounds = 5 in./12.75 cm square

PATTERN NOTES

- Pattern is worked in sections: Back (Granny Square), Sleeves (rounds), Neck Pleat (row).
- Neck Pleat added last along one of the last Granny Square sides, creating a pleat in the fabric to help keep shrug on the shoulders without falling.
- For the best fit, measure between shoulders (across back) and follow pattern with back square at least 4 in./10.25 cm larger for fitted style and up to 10 in./25.5 cm larger for oversize style.

INSTRUCTIONS: Small (Medium, Large)

Back

Follow Granny Square instructions on page 7 until 17 (20, 23) rounds are complete, adding 16 sts to each new round of work, ending with 280 (328, 376) sts; 4 ch-3 spaces + 204 (240, 276) dc + 64 (76, 88) ch-1 spaces.

Do not fasten off; continue to Sleeves.

Sleeves

Sl st into each of next 2 dc, Sl st into ch-3 space.

Round 1: Ch 3 (first dc, here and throughout), work 2 dc into same ch-3 space, ch 1 (3 dc, ch 1) into next 17 (20, 23) ch spaces across, Sl st into top of beginning ch-3 to join—72 (84, 96) sts; 54 (63, 72) dc + 18 (21, 24) ch-1 spaces.

Round 2: Sl st into each of next 2 dc, Sl st into ch-1 space, ch 3, work 2 dc into same ch space, ch 1 (3 dc, ch 1) into each ch-1 space around, Sl st into top of beginning ch-3 to join—72 (84, 96) sts; 54 (63, 72) dc + 18 (21, 24) ch-1 spaces.

Repeat Round 2 until 8 rounds are complete, fasten off.

With right side of Granny Square facing, attach yarn into next unworked ch-3 space from last round of Granny Square.

Repeat rounds 1–8 for Sleeve instructions.

Neck Pleat

Measuring across just one side of last Granny Square round:

Skip 10 in./25.5 cm from right ch-3 corner, place 1 st marker.

Skip 10 in./25.5 cm from left ch-3 corner, place 1 st marker.

Row 1: Sl st into first st marker, [skip 1 st, Sl st into next] until second st marker is reached, fasten off.

Finishing

Sew in all ends, trim excess.

Button Front Top

FINISHED MEASUREMENTS
Small: 32 in./81.25 bust x 16 in./40.75 cm long
Medium: 38 in./96.5 cm bust x 19 in./48.25 cm long
Large: 45 in./114.25 cm bust x 22 in./56 cm long
XLarge: 51 in./129.5 cm bust x 26 in./66 cm long
XXLarge: 58 in./147.25 cm bust x 29 in./73.75 cm long

YARN
Lion Brand Yarn 24/7 Cotton, medium #4 weight (100% mercerized cotton; 3.5 oz./100 g; 186 yds./170 m):
Hay Bale, 2 (2, 3, 4, 5) skeins

HOOK AND OTHER MATERIALS
US M-13 (9.0 mm) crochet hook
Yarn needle
Four 0.75 in./2 cm buttons

GAUGE
3 Granny Square rounds = 5 in./12.75 cm square

SPECIALTY STITCH AND TECHNIQUE
Sew (whipstitch) = Use yarn needle to join (sew) fabric together.

PATTERN NOTES
- Pattern is worked in sections: Back (Granny Square), Front (rows).
- For the best fit, measure around bust at largest point and follow pattern with bust at least 4 in./10.25 cm larger for fitted style and up to 10 in./25.5 cm larger for oversize style.
- Front, Row 1, includes only 3 sides of the Granny Square.

INSTRUCTIONS: Small (Medium, Large, XLarge, XXLarge)

Back
Follow Granny Square instructions on page 7 until 8 (10, 12, 14, 16) rounds are complete, adding 16 sts to each new round of work, ending with 136 (168, 200, 232, 264) sts; 4 ch-3 spaces + 96 (120, 144, 168, 192) dc + 28 (36, 44, 52, 60) ch-1 spaces.
Do not fasten off; continue to Front.

Front

Sl st into each of next 2 dc, Sl st into ch-3 space.

Row 1: Ch 3 (first dc), work 2 dc into same ch-3 space, (ch 1, 3 dc) into each of next 3 (4, 5, 6, 7) ch-1 spaces, ch 17 (21, 25, 29, 33), skip the next 4 (5, 6, 7, 8) ch-1 spaces, (3 dc, ch 1) into each of next 8 (10, 12, 14, 16) ch spaces, 3 dc into next ch-3 space, ch 17 (21, 25, 29, 33), skip the next 4 (5, 6, 7, 8) ch-1 spaces, 3 dc into next ch space, (ch 1, 3 dc) into each of next 3 (4, 5, 6, 7) ch spaces—99 (123, 147, 171, 195) sts; 51 (63, 75, 87, 99) dc + 14 (18, 22, 26, 30) ch-1 spaces + 34 (42, 50, 58, 66) Sleeve chs.

Row 2: Ch 4 (first dc + ch 1), turn, skip 2 dc, [(3 dc, ch 1) into next ch, skip 3 sts] across row, dc into last st of row—99 (123, 147, 171, 195) sts; 74 (92, 110, 128, 146) dc + 25 (31, 37, 43, 49) ch-1 spaces.

Row 3: Ch 3 (first dc), turn, work 2 dc into same ch space, (ch 1, 3 dc) into each ch-1 space across—99 (123, 147, 171, 195) sts; 75 (93, 111, 129, 147) dc + 24 (30, 36, 42, 48) ch-1 spaces.

Row 4: Ch 4 (first dc + ch 1), turn, (3 dc, ch 1) into each ch-1 space across, work 1 dc into last st of row—99 (123, 147, 171, 195) sts; 74 (92, 110, 128, 146) dc + 25 (31, 37, 43, 49) ch-1 spaces.

Repeat rows 3 and 4 until 12 (14, 16, 18, 20) rows are complete.

Do not fasten off; continue to Button Row.

Button Row: Ch 1 (not a st), turn, work 1 sc into each of next 30 (33, 36, 39, 42) sts, fasten off 36 in./91.5 cm tail end—30 (33, 36, 39, 42) sc.

Finishing

With yarn needle, thread 36 in./91.5 cm tail end from Button Row.

Hold Button Row together evenly with last row of Front (opposite Button Row); evenly sew, fasten off.

With right side of Granny Square on the outside (facing), evenly space buttons along Button Row. With yarn, knot each one into place.

Sew in all ends, trim excess.

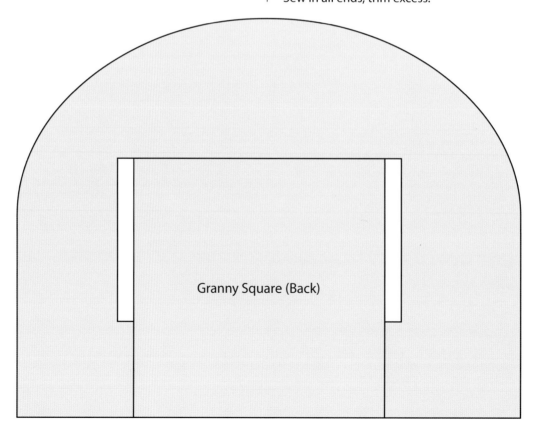

Granny Square (Back)

Basic Stitch Poncho

FINISHED MEASUREMENTS
Around (bust) measures 2 Granny Squares diagonally.
Small: 50 in./127 cm around x 25 in./63.5 cm long
Medium: 55 in./139.75 cm around x 27.5 in./69.75 cm long
Large: 60 in./152.5 cm around x 30 in./76.25 cm long
XLarge: 65 in./165 cm around x 32.5 in./82.5 cm long
XXLarge: 70 in./177.75 cm around x 35 in./90 cm long

YARN
Lion Brand Yarn Basic Stitch Anti-Microbial Thick &
Quick, bulky #5 weight (65% recycled polyester, 35%
Amicor acrylic; 3.5 oz./100 g; 87 yds./80 m): Hazelwood,
6 (6, 7, 8, 8) skeins

HOOK AND OTHER MATERIALS
US M-13 (9.0 mm) crochet hook
Yarn needle

GAUGE
3 Granny Square rounds = 5 in./12.75 cm square
10 Shoulder rows = 4.5 in./11.5 cm

SPECIALTY STITCH AND TECHNIQUE
Sew (whipstitch) = Use yarn needle to join (sew)
pieces of fabric together as described on page 10.

PATTERN NOTES
- Pattern is worked in sections: Granny Square (Front/
  Back), Shoulder (rows).
- For the best fit, measure around arms and torso
  at largest point and follow pattern with bust at
  least 4 in./10.25 cm larger for fitted style and up to
  10 in./25.5 cm larger for oversize style.
- Rows of Shoulder section create head opening,
  which should measure 29 (29, 31, 31, 33) in./
  73.75 (73.75, 78.75, 78.75, 83.75) cm around.

INSTRUCTIONS: Small (Medium, Large, XLarge, XXLarge)

Granny Square (make 2)

Follow Granny Square instructions on page 7 until 10 (11, 12, 13, 14) rounds are complete, adding 16 sts to each new round of work, ending with 168 (184, 200, 216, 232) sts; 4 ch-3 spaces + 120 (132, 144, 156, 168) dc + 36 (40, 44, 48, 52) ch-1 spaces.

Do not fasten off; continue to Shoulder.

Shoulder

Sl st into each of next 4 sts until second ch in next ch-3 space is reached.

Row 1: Ch 1 (not a st), sc, [ch 1, skip 1 st, sc] until second ch in next ch-3 space is reached—43 (47, 51, 55, 59) sts; 22 (24, 26, 28, 30) sc + 21 (23, 25, 27, 29) ch-1 spaces.

Row 2: Ch 1 (not a st), turn, sc, [ch 1, skip 1 st, sc] across row—43 (47, 51, 55, 59) sts; 22 (24, 26, 28, 30) sc + 21 (23, 25, 27, 29) ch-1 spaces.

Repeat row 2 until 34 (34, 36, 36, 38) rows are complete, fasten off leaving a 50 in./127 cm tail.

FINISHING

Hold Granny Square 1 on top of Granny Square 2 with wrong sides together (and right sides facing out).

Thread 50 in./127 cm tail end from shoulder of Granny Square 1; evenly sew last row of shoulder along side 4 of Granny Square 2 (from ch-3 space to ch-3 space).

Thread 50 in./127 cm tail end from shoulder of Granny Square 2; evenly sew last row of shoulder along side 4 of Granny Square 1 (from ch-3 space to ch-3 space).

Sew in all ends, trim excess.

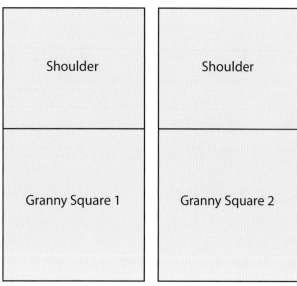

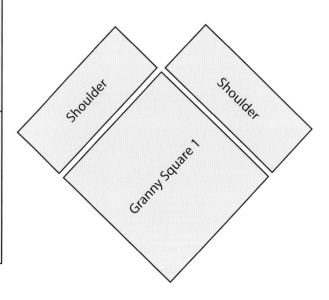

Side-Split Top

FINISHED MEASUREMENTS

Bust measures 2 Granny Squares flat.
Small: 38 in./96.5 cm bust x 19 in./48.25 cm long
Medium: 42 in./106.75 cm bust x 21 in./53.25 cm long
Large: 46 in./116.75 cm bust x 23 in./58.5 cm long
XLarge: 50 in./127 cm bust x 25 in./63.5 cm long
XXLarge: 54 in./137.25 cm bust x 27 in./68.5 cm long

YARN

Lion Brand Yarn Coboo, light #3 weight (51% cotton, 49% rayon from bamboo; 3.5 oz./100 g; 232 yds./ 212 m): Russet, 3 (4, 4, 5, 5) skeins; also shown in Mauve, Pale Pink, Vanilla Blossom, and Lion Brand Yarn Truboo, Khaki

HOOK AND OTHER MATERIALS

US G-6 (4.0 mm) crochet hook
Yarn needle

GAUGE

8 Granny Square rounds = 4 in./10.25 cm square

SPECIALTY STITCHES AND TECHNIQUES

JAYGO (join as you go) = Replace 1 chain stitch with 1 slip stitch into the joining motif as described on page 8.

PATTERN NOTES

- Pattern is worked in sections: Granny Squares (Front/ Back), Shoulders (rows), Neck (rounds), Sleeves (rounds).
- The sides (from the armpit down) are intentionally left open.
- For the best fit, measure around bust at largest point and follow pattern with bust at least 4 in./10.25 cm larger for fitted style, and up to 10 in./25.5 cm larger for oversize style.

Worked in Mauve, Pale Pink, Vanilla Blossom, and Khaki

INSTRUCTIONS: Small (Medium, Large, XLarge, XXLarge)

Granny Square (make 2)

Follow Granny Square instructions on page 7 until 19 (21, 23, 25, 27) rounds are complete, adding 16 sts to each new round of work, ending with 312 (344, 376, 408, 440) sts; 4 ch-3 spaces + 228 (252, 276, 300, 324) dc + 72 (80, 88, 96, 104) ch-1 spaces.

Do not fasten off; continue to Shoulders.

Shoulders

Work Tab 1 and Tab 2 for each Granny Square.

Tab 1

Sl st into each of next 2 dc, Sl st into ch-3 space.

Row 1: Ch 3 (first dc), work 2 dc into same ch-3 space, (ch 1, 3 dc) into each of next 3 (4, 5, 6, 7) ch-1 spaces—15 (19, 23, 27, 31) sts; 12 (15, 18, 21, 24) dc + 3 (4, 5, 6, 7) ch-1 spaces.

Row 2: Ch 4 (first dc + ch 1), turn, (3 dc, ch 1) into each ch-1 space across, work 1 dc into top of last st, fasten off—15 (19, 23, 27, 31) sts; 14 (18, 22, 26, 30) dc + 4 (5, 6, 7, 8) ch-1 spaces.

Tab 2

With right side of Granny Square facing, skip 12 ch-1 spaces after Shoulder Tab 1, row 1, attach yarn into next ch-1 space.

Row 1: Ch 3 (first dc), work 2 dc into same ch-1 space, (ch 1, 3 dc) into each ch space across side including corner ch-3 space—15 (19, 23, 27, 31) sts; 12 (15, 18, 21, 24) dc + 3 (4, 5, 6, 7) ch-1 spaces.

Row 2: Ch 4 (first dc + ch 1), turn, (3 dc, ch 1) into each ch-1 space across, work 1 dc into top of last st, fasten off—15 (19, 23, 27, 31) sts; 14 (18, 22, 26, 30) dc + 4 (5, 6, 7, 8) ch-1 spaces.

Ensure right sides of Granny Squares are facing the same direction.

With a yarn needle, evenly sew the last row of Tab 1 to the last row of Tab 2 for each side for each Granny Square (see diagram on page 31).

Sewing Tabs together creates an opening for the head.

Neck

With right sides of Granny Squares facing, attach yarn into side of any Tab row, on the interior of the Neck opening.

Round 1 (right side): Ch 1 (not a st, here and throughout), work 3 sc into sides of dc sts for each Tab row, work 1 sc into each st across last rows of Granny Square, Sl st into first sc to join—126 sc.

Round 2: Ch 1, work 1 sc into each st around, Sl st into first sc to join—126 sc.

Repeat round 2 once more until 3 rounds are complete. Fasten off.

Worked in Russet

Sleeves

With right side of Granny Squares facing and neck opening centered vertically, work across long side (see bottom diagram).

Beginning with far right ch-3 corner, skip 13 ch spaces, attach yarn into 14th.

Round 1 (right side): Ch 3 (first dc, here and throughout), work 2 dc into same ch space, (ch 1, 3 dc) each of next 6 (8, 10, 12, 14) ch spaces, skip 1 Tab row, (ch 1, 3 dc) into each of next two Tab rows, skip 1 Tab row, (ch 1, 3 dc) into ch-3 space of next Granny Square then into each of next 6 (8, 10, 12, 14) ch spaces, ch 1, Sl st into top of beginning ch-3 to join—64 (80, 96, 112, 128) sts; 48 (60, 72, 84, 96) dc + 16 (20, 24, 28, 32) ch.

Round 2: Sl st into each of next 2 dc, Sl st into ch-1 space, ch 3, work 2 dc into same ch, ch 1, (3 dc, ch 1) into each ch-1 space around, Sl st into top of beginning ch-3 to join—64 (80, 96, 112, 128) sts; 48 (60, 72, 84, 96) dc + 16 (20, 24, 28, 32) ch.

Repeat Round 2 until 4 rounds are complete.

Round 5: Ch 1 (not a st, here and throughout), work 1 sc into each st around—64 (80, 96, 112, 128) sc.

Repeat round 5 until 7 rounds are complete, fasten off.

Finishing

Sew in all ends, trim excess.

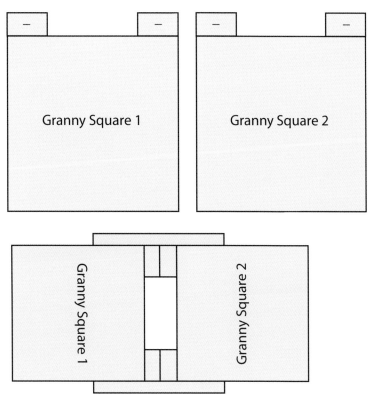

Resources

YarnSub.com—A free site where yarn substitution is made easy!

YouTube.com/AmericanCrochetAssociation—A free library of video tutorials for crochet stitches and other basics like holding your yarn and hook, the slip knot, the slip stitch, color changes, weaving and sewing in ends, and much more!

Ravelry.com/designers/salena-baca—Got a question about one of these designs, or just want to see how others have worked them up? You can find this book, and all the designs, neatly listed on Ravelry with direct access to Salena Baca!

Get started on your next crochet project with one of these great titles, also from Salena Baca:

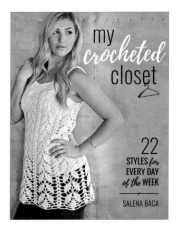

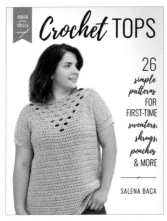